LEADERS OF THE PEOPLE

Other books in the REAL LIVES series

Baseball Greats
Great Adventurers
Heroes & Idealists
Seekers of Truth
Women of Valor

LEADERS OF THE POPLE

edited by
Miriam Rinn

Cover illustration by Warren Chang

Copyright © 1999 by Troll Communications L.L.C.

All rights reserved. No part of this book may be reproduced or utilized in any form or by any means, electronic or mechanical, including photocopying, recording, or by any information storage and retrieval system, without written permission from the publisher.

Printed in the United States of America.   ISBN 0-8167-4929-9

10 9 8 7 6 5 4 3 2 1

TABLE OF CONTENTS

Elizabeth I 9

Patrick Henry 19

Benito Juárez 31

Sitting Bull 43

Theodore Roosevelt 51

Index 62

Elizabeth I

The night sky glowed golden red over London as light blazed from hundreds of bonfires throughout the city. Church bells rang out, and there was dancing and feasting in almost every street in the English capital as the joyous cry of "Long live Princess Elizabeth!" echoed through the night. The celebration, on September 7, 1533, honored the birth of Princess Elizabeth, daughter of King Henry VIII and Queen Anne Boleyn.

There were special reasons for the grand celebration. First of all, Elizabeth was a strong and healthy baby, and that was certainly a reason for great joy. In those days of little medical knowledge, many babies died at birth, and only the strongest survived.

Then, Elizabeth was a truly English princess, and that was another cause for joy. King Henry already had a daughter, 17-year-old Mary, but Catherine, Mary's mother and King Henry's first wife, was Spanish, which meant Mary was half-English and half-Spanish. England and Spain were great rivals, and the English people were afraid of being ruled by a half-Spanish queen. If Mary became queen, would she be loyal to England or Spain? Would she make England a colony of Spain? Would she destroy centuries of English history? Those questions hung over England like a cloud.

Now there was an all-English princess, and there could never be a doubt of her loyalty to her country and people!

King Henry had also longed for a truly English heir, but he did not join in the celebration on the night of Elizabeth's birth. In fact, he was furious and his anger was felt throughout Windsor Castle. Henry had wanted a son, and his astrologers had promised him one. Astrologers studied the positions of the stars and believed such positions influenced events on Earth. The astrologers' predictions, though not scientific, were taken seriously by many people at the time, and Henry was no exception.

The king raged at everyone in sight. He blamed his astrologers. He also blamed his royal advisers, saying they should have stopped him from divorcing Catherine and marrying Anne. Most of all, he blamed Anne for failing to give him the son he wanted.

Nobody could tell how King Henry would act from one minute to the next. First, he was furious about Elizabeth's birth, then he arranged a magnificent christening ceremony and enjoyed every moment of it. A day later, he exploded with fury at having to pay for the feast after the christening. These swift changes of mood made life difficult for everyone around the king, especially his family, so it was lucky for Elizabeth that she did not see her father very often.

The custom of the time was to raise royal children apart from their parents. The royal nursery wasn't even in the same castle as the king and queen's. Right from birth, Elizabeth had her own large staff of servants. There was a lady governess, who was in charge. There were yeomen, the young noblemen who acted as servants to the young princess. There were grooms to care for the horses in Elizabeth's stables. There were officers of the pantry, who bought and prepared food for Elizabeth and her household. There were even three people whose job it was to rock the royal cradle.

There were also two nurses. The choice of nurses was very important, for in those days it was believed that a baby would pick up all the faults, as well as the virtues, of the nurse. There was no work for a cross-eyed nurse or one with an odd voice because people believed the baby would "catch" cross-eye, an odd voice, or any other problem the nurse suffered. A royal nurse was watched every minute. People thought that what you ate shaped your temper and behavior, so the nurse had to eat things that would supposedly make her sweet and proper. The baby in her care would then grow up with these admired qualities.

Strict rules were supposed to protect the royal baby's health. Royal servants were not allowed to go into the city of London, and Londoners who came to deliver food, tools, fabrics, and other merchandise were not allowed inside the walls of the castle. They did all their trading through an iron grille in the castle gate. The great fear of the time was the plague, a disease caused by bacteria. Plague-causing bacteria are carried by fleas, which pass on the disease when they bite humans or animals. Plague is rare in the modern world, but in Elizabeth's time, it was a terrifying and mysterious force. When it struck, it wiped out thousands of people at a time.

Although the royal household tried to guard against this disease, nothing they did could have stopped the plague. People at that time did not know that the illness was carried by fleas, so they paid no attention to cleanliness. Sixteenth-century Europeans had no idea that it was important to bathe and to keep their homes clean. Even the royal nursery was filthy. Fleas were everywhere, on the dogs and cats that wandered freely through the rooms, and on the humans who cared for the infant princess. Princess Elizabeth, like babies through England, had red flea bites on her face and body.

Fleas weren't the only health problem. Stone castles were cold, damp, and drafty. Adults wore heavy clothing, even with fur, indoors and out, and still, coughs and colds were common.

The royal castle also had a terrible smell. There were no

bathrooms and no running water, and garbage was left to rot outside the royal kitchen. Children and grown-ups walked around with flowers or perfumed handkerchiefs, sniffing at these sweet-smelling objects to mask the smell of sewage.

When the stench and filth became unbearable, the royal household packed up and moved. Sometimes, they would move to another royal castle, but other times, they would pay a long visit to the home of a duke or earl. Of course, it was a great honor to entertain the king, but a royal visitor brought servants and soldiers, horses, dogs, clowns, doctors, musicians—a huge crowd. The nobleman was expected to feed and house everyone. It was a very expensive honor!

When the royal family left one of their castles, every room was cleaned. In fact, this was the only time a castle was aired and scrubbed.

Even though she was surrounded by dirt and disease, Elizabeth grew into a healthy, pretty child. She had beautiful coloring—rosy cheeks, a clear and creamy skin, and bright red hair. The pretty princess was a delight to the English people. Elizabeth was also fortunate to have a good governess, Lady Margaret Bryan. Lady Bryan was as kind to Elizabeth as if she were the child's own mother. That was a good thing, because Elizabeth had so little to do with her parents. As a matter of fact, when she talked about it years later, she could remember being with both of them only two times.

The first was a happy occasion, when Elizabeth was two and a half years old. Queen Anne was going to have a baby, and King Henry told everyone this child would be a boy. He was so sure of this that he even gave a huge party where the king wore shiny yellow clothes and had Princess Elizabeth dressed in a matching yellow gown.

Elizabeth never forgot that party. Her tall, powerful father carried her around, showing her off to everyone and calling her the prettiest lass in the world. The second occasion Elizabeth remembered was an unhappy one. When the son Henry wanted was born dead, the king turned his fury against the queen and had her put on trial for treason. The royal councilors found her guilty, and the king ordered her to be beheaded.

Several days before the execution, Queen Anne made a last plea for her life. A nobleman who was present later wrote these words to Elizabeth: "Alas, I shall never forget the sorrow I felt when I saw the sainted queen, your mother. She was carrying you in her arms. She came to the most serene king, your father, in Greenwich Palace. She brought you to him in the courtyard as he stood at the open window. She begged for her life to be spared for your sake."

The king would not change his mind, and Anne was put to death in the Tower of London. Just one day later, King Henry married Jane Seymour, who he hoped would give birth to a healthy son to inherit the throne.

Elizabeth became a forgotten princess. The king did not want to see her or hear her name. In time, she outgrew the clothes her mother, Queen Anne, had bought for her, but no new ones were made. Finally, Lady Bryan sent a letter to the king begging for dresses, shoes, petticoats, nightgowns, and other articles of clothing for the princess. King Henry's secretary sent a small amount of money and included a letter telling Lady Bryan not to ask again. Elizabeth, he wrote, was to live without luxuries. Her mother had angered the king, and for this reason the child must suffer too.

Elizabeth's life changed again when she was four years old. Queen Jane gave birth to a boy, who was named Edward. The king was so pleased that he even allowed Elizabeth to be treated better. She was dressed in fine clothes again and given a larger staff of servants, 32 in all. A new governess, Katherine Champernowne, replaced Lady Bryan. Again, Elizabeth was lucky—her new governess was a well-educated woman and an excellent teacher.

Princess Elizabeth was a very bright child. By the time she was six, she could read and write as well as most adults of that time, and she also knew Latin. In addition to Katherine Champernowne, the young princess had several teachers. One taught her mathematics, another taught her Italian and French, and still others taught her music, art, and dancing.

There were no textbooks so the Bible was used for teaching. Elizabeth first learned to read the Bible, then she learned to write by copying lines from the Bible. She read the Bible in Latin and learned to translate Biblical passages from Latin into English and from English into French.

The young princess did read other books, but not many. There were no children's books then, so the books Elizabeth read were always very serious. Sixteenth-century children were brought up strictly. A philosopher of that time wrote that laughter meant empty-headedness or wickedness. A proper child, he said, might smile a bit, but not much nor for very long. Also, when a child laughed, the mouth should be covered by a handkerchief.

Laughter wasn't the only thing to be avoided by children. They were also told not to wrinkle the nose, twist the mouth, frown, yawn, sniffle, or sneeze. They must not jump around, play, or act like children at all. Children were considered to be small adults, and they were expected to act like adults. When children acted like children, they were called wicked, and the punishment for being wicked could be very severe.

Princess Elizabeth had more reason than most children to fear punishment. King Henry did nothing to control his anger, and when he was angry enough, he sent people to prison or to be executed. He did not even spare his own family. Of King Henry's six wives, two he divorced and banished from England, and two he had executed. Another died during childbirth. Only his sixth and last wife, Catherine Parr, outlived him—by a year.

King Henry's violence made a deep impression on Princess Elizabeth. She grew up afraid to trust anyone, and she never let anyone become close to her. Many times when Elizabeth was queen, it looked as if she might marry, but each time she changed her mind, offering a reason for turning down the proposal of marriage. If she married a foreign king, Elizabeth said, it might be bad for England. A foreigner could make England a colony of his own country. Many English people agreed with Elizabeth, and they accepted this explanation.

The English people wanted Elizabeth to marry an Englishman, and they wanted her to have children. If Elizabeth didn't have children, who would rule England when she died? Would the French, Spanish, or Scottish take over? Would there be wars fought over the English throne?

Elizabeth understood the fears of her people, but her own fear was greater. Any husband, English or foreign, might try to take the throne from her, since women, even queens, had almost no rights. He might even condemn her to death, as her father had done to her mother. This fear ruled the queen of England as strongly as she ruled her country.

Elizabeth's feelings were not surprising. Until she became queen, she never really felt safe. Before King Henry died in 1547, there was always the danger of his anger. After Henry's death, nine-year-old Prince Edward became king. He was a nice boy and liked his 13-year-old half-sister, Elizabeth, but because he was still a child, he had no real power. England was actually ruled by Edward's uncles and cousins. They were not related to Elizabeth and did not feel any loyalty to her. Elizabeth wasn't mistreated by them, but she still lived in fear. Wisely, the teenage princess tried not to be noticed too much.

Elizabeth stayed in the country, far from London, where her days were filled with study. The finest professors from Cambridge University were happy to teach the brilliant princess. Elizabeth spoke and read French, Italian, Latin, Greek, and Spanish, as well as her native English. She knew a great deal of mathematics and science. She wrote music, played more than one musical instrument, and sang in a clear, sweet voice.

Elizabeth did not think she would ever be queen. Still, she loved her country and had dreams of glory for England, so she studied the art of government with special care. She studied geography and imagined English colonies in the New World. She studied military history and dreamed of a mighty English navy that would rule the seas. In the quiet of her country home, Elizabeth dedicated herself to learning and thinking, and those years of intense study would one day be put to good use.

In 1553, 15-year-old King Edward VI died. Who would take the throne of England? Just before the young king's death, he was convinced to name a cousin, Lady Jane Grey, as his successor, and she declared herself queen the day he died.

Princess Elizabeth did nothing, but her older half-sister, Mary, acted. Refusing to accept Lady Jane Grey as the new queen, Mary gathered an army and overthrew Lady Jane's government. In August 1553, Mary Tudor became queen of England.

Many of the English people did not want Mary on the throne. She was half-Spanish and a Roman Catholic, and this bothered them. It bothered them even more when Mary married Prince Philip of Spain. The threat of Spanish conquest was growing every day, and more and more English people wanted Elizabeth as their queen. When Mary learned of the young princess's popularity, she accused Elizabeth of plotting to overthrow the government.

Elizabeth was not involved in any plot, and she told Mary so, in letters and in person. Mary, who had waited many years to become queen, was furious at Elizabeth's popularity, and she had no intention of letting her pretty half-sister take the crown from her now. In March 1554, two councilors came to escort Elizabeth to prison in the Tower of London. Shocked, Elizabeth asked to be brought to the queen, but Mary would not see her. Elizabeth then wrote a letter to Mary, saying that she was innocent and faithful to the throne.

The letter covered a page and a half, and where nothing was written, Elizabeth drew slanting lines. This, she explained, was to make sure that nobody could write bad things and say that they were her words. It was clever of Elizabeth to do this, but not surprising. She had been well trained not to trust messengers, councilors, or even relatives.

The letter did no good. The 20-year-old Elizabeth was taken to the Tower, and to make things worse, she was brought in through the Traitor's Gate. Only condemned prisoners were taken to the Tower that way. It was a terrible disgrace for Elizabeth.

She remained in the Tower for two months, fearing her execution would take place any day. Mary did not dare to have her sister killed, however, for she feared that the English might rise up in rebellion if the well-loved Elizabeth was put to death. Instead, Mary freed Elizabeth and sent her off to the country.

In November 1558, Mary died, and Elizabeth's life of fear finally ended. When she became queen of England, all her years of preparation proved of value. For the full length of her long reign, lasting until her death in 1603, England flourished and became the most powerful nation on earth. Under Elizabeth, a powerful English navy destroyed the Spanish fleet in 1588, and with it Spain's place as a major force among nations.

Elizabeth also encouraged her navy to range far and wide, to explore the known and unknown world. These explorations led to the development of colonies in North America. In a sense, American history began during the reign of Queen Elizabeth I.

Elizabeth's years on the throne are important for other reasons. England enjoyed many years of prosperity and peace during her reign, and she encouraged the arts as no ruler had before her. It was an age when the writing of plays and poetry blossomed. William Shakespeare, one of the greatest writers of all time, produced his masterpieces during the Elizabethan Age. In fact, a number of his plays were specifically written for the queen to see.

Queen Elizabeth I died on March 24, 1603. In the 45 years she ruled England, she accomplished great things. The England she began to rule in 1558 was just a small island, always in danger from other countries. The England she left was a far-reaching power. Queen Elizabeth I planted the seeds that would grow into the British Empire—an island nation that at one time ruled almost half the world!

Patrick Henry

May 29, 1736 was a golden spring day. The sun warmed the green fields and sent bright arrows of light through treetops to the forest floor below. The colony of Virginia was a rich land, with plentiful wild game in the woods, clear mountain streams, fertile farmland, and a world of opportunity for its citizens. Anyone born in such a place at that time could look forward to a full and happy future.

This was just the way Sarah and John Henry felt as they looked at their newborn baby, a sturdy, round-faced boy with a shock of red hair and sparkling blue eyes. He also had a loud, healthy cry, which filled the room.

"Young Patrick is well named," said Mrs. Henry, laughing.

"Indeed," Mr. Henry agreed. "His voice is the equal of my brother Patrick's. And do you think he will one day be a minister, like his namesake?"

"Heaven knows if he'll be delivering sermons," said Mrs. Henry, "but one thing is certain—people will be sure to hear him!"

Little Patrick quieted down soon enough. A bright boy who didn't say much, he watched and listened very closely. He would sit quietly, his face serious, taking in every word spoken by the adults around him. Patrick heard his father tell about the old days in Scotland, of the poverty he saw when he lived in Aberdeen, and of the dreams that had brought him from the land of his birth to Colonial America. In 1707, Scotland had become part of the British empire, but many Scots, like the fiercely proud Henrys, resented their English rulers. They wanted to have their own laws, their own church, their own king.

Patrick listened to his father talk with pride about his family, and how they had fought against the British crown. The Henrys had a strong tradition—they stood up for what they felt was right, no matter how harsh the penalty.

Hanover County, Virginia, was the home of many emigrants from Scotland, and from them, Patrick learned many of the customs and ways of his Highland ancestors. He learned to play hard and work hard, never to back off from a fight, never to waste a penny, and always to be fair in his dealings with others. One of the customs that Patrick enjoyed most was the yearly celebration of Saint Andrew's Day, in honor of the patron saint of Scotland, held in the town of Hanover Courthouse every fall.

Patrick always looked forward to this fun-filled day with its contests and prizes. The winning boxer won a hat worth twenty shillings, the winning wrestler got a pair of silver shoe buckles, the finest dancer got a pair of handsome shoes, and the prettiest young woman got a pair of expensive silk stockings. A race brought together the 20 fastest horses in the county. There was a drum-playing contest, with the rule that no drummer could beat the drum with his left hand. There was a singing competition, and 20 of the county's best fiddlers entered in a contest, with the top player winning a brand-new fiddle.

Patrick loved the sound of old Scottish tunes played by the fiddlers. In fact, the music pleased him so much that he just had to learn to play the fiddle himself. When Mr. and Mrs. Henry saw that he had a good ear for music, they gave him a violin. That was all the youngster needed, and on his own, he taught himself country fiddling. When he was a teenager he also taught himself to play the flute, the lute, and the harpsichord. The joy of making music would stay with Patrick Henry all his life. Years later, when he had his own family, they would sit in the parlor and sing hymns every Sunday evening while Patrick's violin accompanied their voices.

The Saint Andrew's Day festivities reached their peak for the youngsters in the late afternoon. As the banquet tables were being set up, sides of beef, wild turkeys, pigs, chickens, and ducks were roasted over roaring fires. Women unpacked hampers filled with pies, puddings, vegetables, fresh-baked breads, and other tasty foods.

While all this was going on, there were footraces for the boys. Year after year, Patrick was among the fastest runners in Hanover County, and when he was eight, he had his best running year. He won the Saint Andrew's Day race for boys between ages seven and nine, and his prize was a piping hot mince pie, which he proudly shared with his family.

Young Patrick had a good time all year long. On some days he would get together with one or two friends, and they would take their fishing poles to one of the many creeks around Hanover Courthouse. On other days he would go hunting with his father and his older brothers, John and William.

In those days, hunting was not just a sport. The game the Henrys shot might be the next day's dinner, or it might be cured and stored for next winter. Patrick enjoyed hunting all his life, but it was as much for the quiet and beauty of the woods as for the game he brought home. From childhood on, Patrick loved to wander alone in the woods. He could sit for hours at a time, watching the animals. He was especially interested in birds, listening to them chirp and sing, then imitating their songs.

Most people were amused by Patrick's clever bird imitations, but some folks in Hanover Courthouse called him "that lazy Henry boy," for spending so much time doing "nothing worthwhile." His parents didn't agree. They felt that Patrick was a good boy, and not the least bit lazy when they had something for him to do.

For most children growing up in Virginia in the 1700s, schooling ended when they were about 10 or 11 years old. Book learning was not considered necessary to be a farmer, a storekeeper, or just about anything else. Patrick's education did not end, however, when he stopped going to school. His father became his full-time teacher, and Mr. Henry gave his son a hard course of study for the next five years. John Henry, who had spent four years at Aberdeen University, was a good teacher, and as Samuel Meredith, Patrick's friend and neighbor, wrote later, "Patrick acquired a knowledge of the Latin language and a smattering of the Greek. He became well acquainted with mathematics, of which he was very fond. At the age of 15, he was well versed in both ancient and modern history."

Meredith also remembered Patrick as being a quiet, thoughtful boy. Whenever his friends had an argument, Patrick was the one they turned to for a fair, sensible decision. He would listen very carefully to both sides, then take some time to think the matter over. It seemed he took the longest time for thinking when the argument was a really hot one—enough time for tempers to cool on both sides.

Finally, in a soft, reasonable voice, Patrick would give his opinion. He spoke so well that he almost always made both sides happy with his decisions. More than anything else, this skill—to persuade others through words—earned Patrick a good reputation with the young people in Hanover Courthouse.

Another friend remembered the way Patrick looked as a young teenager. "His face was longish and thin. He had a sharp nose, freckles, and eyes as blue as a jay's wing. And you see Patrick a long way off, with that thatch of hair the color of a ripe pumpkin."

The friend also talked about the way Patrick dressed. "His breeches, coat, and boots were like what we all wore—homespun and plain. But Patrick was different from us in one way. He always tried to keep his shirt and stockings clean. That didn't much matter to the rest of us."

To many of the boys of Hanover Courthouse, Patrick was best known as a practical joker. One time, he caught a young skunk in a trap he had set in the woods. He put the skunk in a straw basket and covered it with a cloth, then brought it to school early one morning and set it on the teacher's desk. The teacher saw the basket and smiled, thinking it was filled with vegetables, fruit, corn, or animal skins. That was the way parents paid for their children's schooling. The teacher would use what he could and sell the rest.

This time, the teacher was in for a surprise. He lifted the cloth cover and saw two beady, black eyes staring up at him. Furious, the teacher roared, "Who put this beast here? I'll whip the scoundrel!" Glaring at the class, the teacher grabbed one of the birch switches he kept near his desk and whipped it against the desktop in rage. The skunk, terrified by the sharp sound, jumped out of the basket, lifted its striped tail, and used its famous weapon. The children flew from the room, the teacher right behind them. School was closed for the rest of that week, and everyone—except the teacher—knew the person to thank for the holiday!

There was no doubt that Patrick had a real gift for talking. His uncle, Isaac Winston, once said, "Patrick, when he speaks, stirs the boys so that I've seen them jump up and crack their heels together, and slam their caps on the ground and stamp them."

Isaac's brother, William Winston, was also a fine talker, and his oratory impressed young Patrick deeply. The boy began by copying his Uncle Billy and soon was the better speaker. Uncle Billy taught Patrick how to hold the attention of a large group of people, when to speak in quiet tones, when to pause, when to raise his voice dramatically, how to stand, and what to do with his hands as he spoke.

Uncle Billy also taught Patrick the ways of the woods. A true frontiersman, Billy dressed in buckskin, spent half the year hunting deer, and often lived with the Indians. Sometimes he would take Patrick with him into the backwoods for a week or two, where they camped out, Indian-style, living on berries, nuts, and whatever they could hunt or fish.

Being out with Uncle Billy gave Patrick a feeling of independence that he could not get anywhere else. The towns and farms of Virginia were very much like the towns and farms of England and Scotland, just as the habits, clothing, and customs of the people were similar to life in the old country. The colonists had recreated the life they knew. In the wilderness with his uncle, however, Patrick discovered a new America, wild and free. He discovered a new Patrick, as well. He no longer felt like an English subject living far from the mother country. He felt independent and at liberty. These thoughts and feelings were puzzling to the young Virginian. Sometimes he tried to tell Uncle Billy what was in his mind, but he couldn't find the right words.

"I know what you mean," Uncle Billy told Patrick. "I feel it, too, and I know others who feel the same things. The time is coming—soon—when we'll put these feelings into action. And when that time comes, you'll find the right words to say."

Shortly after he turned 15, Patrick got his first real job as a clerk in a country store. The Henry family could not afford to send him to college, but Patrick was already well educated and ready to begin learning a trade.

The store where Patrick worked sold nearly everything the local people didn't grow or make themselves. Customers could buy corks, saddles, snuff, shoes, silk, eyeglasses, books, salt, tea, mirrors, candle molds, needles and threads, buttons, tools, and other useful items. Patrick clerked there for a year, and in that time, he learned to keep the store clean, to wait on customers, and to do any other task the storekeeper set him to. Then, when he was 16, he left the store at his father's suggestion.

"You have done well in your employment," John Henry told his son. "It shows you can succeed at business, and since your brother William is a hard worker, I have in mind that you and he should have your own general store."

"Oh, Father!" Patrick cried. "Do you really think we can do it soon?"

"Yes, I do," Mr. Henry answered. "In fact, I have seen just the place for this store. There is a small house where Newcastle Road meets Old Church Road. Everyone crossing the river must pass that way, and there are people on the roads day and night. With good merchandise and hard work, you and William should do quite well for yourselves. I expect you to pay me back in a very short time."

Mr. Henry rented the small house and stocked it with goods to sell while Patrick and William fixed and cleaned the building, inside and out. They built wooden shelves and a counter, then they hand-lettered signs to hang all around the store. At last, the Henry Brothers General Store was open for trade.

As Mr. Henry had predicted, there were plenty of customers. The boys were kept very busy, but they did not make a profit. In those days, it was common for people to trade for what they needed. Customers paid in money, tobacco, fruits and vegetables they had grown, game they had shot, and fur pelts, then the storekeeper sold the goods his customers used as payment. When they didn't have money or goods to trade, they asked the storekeeper to sell to them on credit and promised to pay as soon as they could.

Patrick, in charge of the store's finances, gave credit to just about anyone who asked, which brought the Henry brothers a lot of customers. The problem was, Patrick did not demand payment, and he always believed the excuses the non-paying customers gave him. With very little money coming in, Patrick and William could not buy new merchandise to stock the shelves, and they could not pay back the amount Mr. Henry had loaned them to open the store. After a year of this, their father made it clear that he would not lend any more money to such bad managers. It came as no surprise when the Henry brothers went out of business.

While Patrick was not a success at business, he gained a great deal from the time he spent in the store. Like many frontier general stores, the Henry brothers' place was a popular meeting spot. People would come in to learn the latest gossip, to talk about their crops and the weather, to swap stories and tall tales, and to argue politics. Patrick was most interested in the political arguments. He was a native-born American, like many of the younger people in the colonies. Unlike the older folks, who came from Great Britain and had strong ties to the old country, the younger people didn't think about Great Britain as "home." The young and the old often disagreed, and the store saw many a lively debate between them—about freedom, about the right of colonists to make their own laws, and about land.

Anyone who rode west could see endless miles of rich country, unsettled and unmapped, but the colonists were not free to live on it. By law, all of this land belonged not to the Native Americans who had been there for thousands of years nor to the colonists who were willing to develop it, but to the king or to noblemen who lived in England. This angered many of the younger colonists.

Because he read so much and knew many facts, Patrick was usually in the middle of the political debates. Because he was such a good talker, he was often one of the main speakers. People who defended the king when they came into the store sometimes left with a very different feeling. Patrick's words and the sense he made changed their opinions.

These debates could have made Patrick many enemies, but the tall, lanky teenager was so likable and clever that nobody took offense at his words. More than one listener told him, "Patrick, you ought to be a lawyer, or maybe you ought to get yourself elected to the House of Burgesses over in Williamsburg."

It was a good prediction of what lay ahead for Patrick Henry. He would become a lawyer, one of the best in the colonies, and one day, in 1765, he would be elected to the House of Burgesses, the colonial legislature of Virginia. There, as the representative from Louisa County, Patrick would stand out as one of the most forceful voices for independence, and, in speaking to this Virginia legislature, he would say the fiery words that would be repeated with admiration throughout the colonies.

Just nine days after Patrick took his seat in the House of Burgesses, he introduced a resolution protesting the Stamp Act, which placed a high tax on the colonies by the British government. The speech he made, defending his resolution, included these famous words, "Caesar had his Brutus, Charles I had his Cromwell, and George III—"

At this moment, the Speaker of the House cried out, "Treason! Treason!" The Speaker was accusing Patrick of treason for saying that King George should be overthrown as Caesar was overthrown by Brutus and Charles I by Cromwell. Those who were present that day remembered how Patrick's blue eyes stared icily at the Speaker, and how he coolly finished his sentence, "—may profit by their example! If this be treason, make the most of it!"

Patrick would make an even more famous—and more important—speech 10 years later. By this time the colonies were on the edge of rebellion against England, and King George III had closed the House of Burgesses, but he couldn't stop the Virginians from meeting and planning their future. The meeting, called the Virginia Convention, was held in Richmond in the spring of 1775. The vote to be taken there would decide if Virginia would support the American Revolution or the king.

The men who spoke against revolution pointed out how war would hurt the colonists. They spoke of the thousands who would die on both sides, saying that American guns would be firing at men who were brothers and cousins. Even at the price of freedom, they called for peace.

When it seemed that these Loyalists might win the vote, Patrick Henry leaped to his feet. The hall fell silent, for nobody on this morning of March 23, 1775, wanted to miss a word uttered by this spellbinding speaker.

Patrick spoke of Virginia's noble history, of the patience the colonists had shown each time the king put a heavier burden on them. He spoke of the efforts made by the House of Burgesses, and how the king had scorned them. Then, with these ringing words, he closed his speech, "Gentlemen may cry peace, peace—but there is no peace. The war is actually begun! The next gale that sweeps the north will bring to our ears the clash of resounding arms. Our brethren are already in the field! Why stand we here idle? What is it the gentlemen wish? What would they have?

"Is life so dear, or peace so sweet, as to be purchased at the price of chains and slavery? Forbid it, almighty God! I know not what course others may take; but as for me—give me liberty or give me death!"

These stirring words led to an overwhelming vote for revolution, and they were echoed again and again throughout the colonies as other Americans joined in the fight for liberty.

Patrick, who also served five terms as governor of Virginia, continued to be a leading force in the war for American independence. When he died, on June 6, 1799, Patrick Henry was honored as the most unforgettable voice of the American Revolution.

Benito Juárez

The first light of day crept over Mexico's Sierra del Sur mountains. The villagers of San Pablo Gualatao were still sleeping—except in the house of Marcelino and Brigida Juárez. Everyone there was awake, getting ready for an important event. The Juárezes' one-day-old son was to be baptized that very afternoon, March 22, 1806, and the baby was to be called Benito Pablo.

Señor Juárez stood at the door, holding the sleeping baby. Maria Josefa and Rosa kissed their new brother and Señora Juárez stroked the baby's soft cheek. "We will wait for your return," she said to her husband. "Go with God."

That afternoon Benito Pablo Juárez was baptized at the tiny village church in Santo Tomas Ixtlan. The family had no money for a celebration or even for a new baby blanket. Señor Juárez gave a few coins—all the money he had—to the priest who baptized the baby, and the Juárezes felt lucky that they were able to do this much for their newborn. Most of the 20 families in their village had no money at all. The lives of everybody in San Pablo Gualatao were a constant struggle against poverty, starvation, and disease.

The Juárez family, like their neighbors, were Zapotec Indians whose ancestors had lived in the mountains of southern Mexico for thousands of years. They were peace-loving, hard-working people who farmed the land and raised sheep. When the Aztecs overran Mexico in the 12th century, they found it difficult to conquer the Zapotecs, and when the Spanish conquistadores invaded Mexico in the 16th century, they met the same stubborn resistance.

The Zapotecs were not an aggressive people who invaded other peoples' territories. They simply defended their own land, but they never gave up. Benito Juárez was born into this tradition of pride, quiet strength, and the will to survive, and it was this tradition that shaped his life and explains Juárez's importance to the shaping of modern Mexico.

Right from the start, life was hard for Benito. As he wrote when he was an adult, "I had the misfortune not to have known my parents . . . for I was hardly three years old when they died, leaving me and my sisters to the care of our paternal grandparents, Pedro Juárez and Justa Lopez, Indians also of the Zapotec nation."

There were no doctors or nurses in San Pablo Gualatao, and Benito's mother had died giving birth to another child. His father had collapsed and died in a marketplace in the city of Oaxaca, after walking 40 miles over the mountains from his village, carrying fruit grown in his small garden. Señor and Señora Juárez were not even 30 years old when they died.

When Benito was six, his grandparents also died, and the three Juárez children were homeless again. Maria Josefa went to Oaxaca, to work as a housemaid. Rosa, who was in her teens, married and moved to a nearby village, and Benito was taken in by his father's brother, Bernardino. Bernardino Juárez owned a small plot of land in the mountains near the Laguna Encantada, "the Enchanted Lake." Despite its name, there was nothing enchanting about the land. It was rocky and steep, with barely enough grass for Uncle Bernardino's small flock of sheep to graze on. Benito was put right to work, doing chores in the house, carrying water from a nearby stream, and helping his uncle tend the flock.

Benito spoke only the Zapotec language, which was fine for talking with family and friends, but the official language of Mexico was Spanish. Without knowing Spanish, there was no way for a person to be anything but a poor peasant. Since there were no schools in any of the Zapotec villages, it was almost impossible for an Indian to break the chains of poverty.

"Our people have lived in this land for thousands of years," Uncle Bernardino told the boy. "Even so, we remain poor and without opportunity. You are smart and learn fast. You must use what God has given you and make your life better. You must learn Spanish. You must learn to read and write. You can be somebody special, Benito. You must not live out your life as a poor uneducated man!"

Bernardino Juárez wanted his nephew to become a priest, the best way for a poor Zapotec boy to get ahead in the world. To be a priest, the boy had to go to a seminary, and to be accepted by the seminary, Benito had to learn Spanish.

Uncle Bernardino knew a little Spanish, and tried to teach it to his nephew. Although Benito wanted to learn, it wasn't easy. It took endless hours of work just to survive because everything the family needed came from their own efforts. Their clothing was made of cloth they wove themselves, the cloth came from thread they spun themselves, and the thread came from the wool of their own sheep.

Every bite of food the Juárezes ate—bananas, prickly pears, brown beans, potatoes, chickpeas—came from their own garden. They ground their own flour to make tortillas, and they harvested honey from their own beehives. Nothing was bought, not even the tools they used to farm the land.

Benito Juárez never forgot what life was like during his childhood. In those years when the crops failed, times were especially hard. The family had to survive on a cactus plant called maguey, which grew in the rocky soil. The maguey's sap was like sugar water, sweet and nourishing to the body. The Juárezes drank the maguey sap and used the rest of the plant in many other ways. They made thread, called pita, from the fibers, and the pita was made into sturdy cloth and paper. Even the thorns did not go to waste, but were used for pins, needles, and nails.

Young Benito and his family were exhausted by sundown, worn out by endless hours of work. There was little time left to learn Spanish, or anything else. Again and again, Bernardino told his nephew, "My greatest wish is for you to go to school, to escape this life. Maybe someday soon it will be possible."

But "someday" never seemed to come any closer for Benito. When he was 10 years old, he was put in charge of his uncle's flock of sheep and spent every day up in the hills overlooking the Enchanted Lake. Lonely and unhappy, Benito passed the time talking to the sheep and dreaming of a better life. There was only one way Benito could think of to escape the endless poverty and make something of his life. As he wrote many years later, "Fathers who could afford the schooling of their children took them to the city of Oaxaca for that purpose. Those who could not pay the fee put the children into service in private homes on condition that they be taught to read and write. This was the only method of education in use, not only in my village, but in the whole district of Ixtlan.

"It was a remarkable fact in that period that most of the servants in the houses in the City were young people from that district. Because of these facts . . . I came to the conclusion that only by going to the City could I learn, and I often begged my uncle to take me to the capital."

Uncle Bernardino always promised to do so, someday, but it was another "someday" that never came. Then, one day, everything changed. On December 16, 1818, 12-year-old Benito was up in the hills watching the flock. Around 11 o'clock that morning, a group of mule-drivers passed by on the road. Benito asked them if they came from Oaxaca, and they said they did. The boy had many questions about the big city, and before they continued on their journey, the men told him wonderful stories of the people, the buildings, and all the grand things that happened there.

When Benito went back to his flock, he noticed that one of the sheep was missing. He scrambled up and down the rocky paths, looking for the lost sheep. Then, as he wrote, "Another shepherd boy approached and told me that he had seen one of the mule-drivers make away with the sheep."

Benito felt stupid at being fooled by the slick-talking men, and he felt guilty for losing a valuable animal. Uncle Bernardino had so little, but he shared everything he owned and always treated Benito like a son. As he sat on the hillside, frightened of being punished and confused, Benito decided to run away. By sunset, as he led the flock home, he had a plan.

The next morning at dawn, Benito sneaked out of his uncle's hut and began walking to Oaxaca. It took all day to cover the 40 miles, and he was hungry, thirsty, and tired when he finally reached the city. There he looked for the house of Don Antonio Maza where Maria Josefa, Benito's big sister, was a cook. She was the only person he knew in the whole city, and he had to find her.

When at last Benito found the Maza house, he told his sister what had happened. She went to Don Antonio, repeated the boy's story, and asked that Benito be allowed to stay there. "My brother is strong and willing to work," Maria Josefa said. "He wants to stay in Oaxaca to go to school. Will you help us?"

Don Antonio agreed to let Benito live in the house until the boy found a permanent place to stay. Benito earned his keep by doing odd jobs for the Maza family, and when he was not working, the boy from the tiny mountain village roamed the streets of Oaxaca. He listened, looked, and learned.

Oaxaca's buildings and gardens were more beautiful than Benito ever imagined. There were marketplaces with endless varieties of vegetables, fruits, meats, cakes, furniture, silks, lace, and silver, and finely dressed people rode in horse-drawn carriages. Before he came to Oaxaca, Benito had only known poor Zapotec Indians living in tiny villages, but now he began to see what other parts of Mexico were like. What he saw was a Mexico cruelly ruled in a way unfair to most of the people. Half of all Mexicans were Native Americans, like the Zapotec, but they were treated more like slaves. Mexico's Native Americans had no rights under the law, no education, and no opportunity to improve their lives.

The next largest group of Mexicans was called mestizo, people who were part Native American and part Spanish. Mestizos were treated better than Native Americans, but they, too, did not have a voice in the way Mexico was run. The next step on the ladder held a smaller group of people called Creoles, descendants of Spanish people, but they were born in Mexico.

The smallest, and most powerful, group in Mexico were people born in Spain. These people ruled Mexico, and they had more legal rights than anyone else. Mexican laws were so biased toward the Spanish born that children born in Mexico to Spanish parents had fewer rights than their parents. For this reason, the laws often turned children and their parents into enemies.

When Benito was a boy, Mexico was still a colony of Spain, and many Mexicans hated Spain the same way the English colonists farther north hated England's rule. Those colonists had declared their independence from England in 1776, and gone on to become the United States of America. Mexicans suffering under the iron rule of Spain longed for the same freedom and independence.

Spain kept a stranglehold on Mexico with a code of strict laws.

Mexicans were not allowed to make or grow anything that was made or grown in Spain, so machines, cloth, tools, and many other manufactured goods had to be bought from Spain. Among the many forbidden crops in Mexico were flax and hemp, which were used to make cloth and rope. Mexicans were not allowed to grow grapes, or the mulberry trees needed to feed the silkworms that make silk. Every ounce of Mexico's greatest wealth—the millions of tons of gold and silver in the mountains—was shipped to Spain to fill the treasury of the Spanish kings.

Mexico received nothing in return for all this gold and silver. Even though there was no legal slavery in the country, most Mexicans lived like slaves, in total, hopeless poverty. This fueled a growing anger, and by the time Benito Juárez reached Oaxaca in 1818, there had been two revolts against the government. Both had been crushed by the army, but that only deepened the people's fury against their rulers.

Mexico was a troubled land when 12-year-old Benito began his education. Don Antonio Maza had found him a place in the home of Don Antonio Salanueva, a kind, intelligent man. He was deeply religious and believed that education was very important, so when his new houseboy, Benito, showed a strong desire to learn, Don Antonio enrolled him in an elementary school.

In the next two years, Benito went through four grades, learning to read and write simple Spanish. Schools for Native Americans were allowed to teach only basic subjects, but Benito wanted to learn more. He begged to be sent to a better school, and Don Antonio agreed. He wanted Benito to become a priest, and that required a real education, so he sent the boy to the Royal School.

Benito was excited to be a new student at the Royal School, but he soon learned that there were two separate sections—one for Native-American boys and one for Spanish and Creole boys. The Native-American class didn't even have a regular teacher, but was taught by an untrained assistant, and when Benito or one of his classmates made a mistake, they were not helped, they were punished.

Years later, Benito Juárez remembered, "I was disgusted with this wretched method of instruction. Since there was no other establishment in the city to which I could go, I decided definitely to leave school, and to practice the little I had learned by myself, until I could express my ideas in writing."

True to his word, Benito spent many hours reading and teaching himself grammar, spelling, and penmanship. Benito's life was not all work, however. He still found some time for fun and friends. Benito and his friends liked to play running and jumping games in the neighborhood, and the boys also found time for pranks, with Benito leading the way. Once, he bought a basket of rotten apples for a few pennies and gave the apples to his friends to use as ammunition. Their target was anyone unlucky enough to be in the marketplace. When Don Antonio heard about this, he was furious and let Benito know it!

Another of Benito's ideas was more acceptable. At a nearby lakefront, he built a diving board, using a barrel and two wooden boards. The first time he tried jumping from it, Benito and the board went into the water together. The next time it worked, and Benito charged other divers to use it. At a few pennies a jump, he made enough to buy a huge bag of candy to share with all his friends.

On October 21, 1821, 15-year-old Benito entered the seminary in Oaxaca. Over the next four years he mastered Spanish and Latin, and in August 1825, he passed his examinations with a grade of "Excellent." Instead of stopping there, he continued his studies at the seminary with advanced classes in philosophy, the arts, religion, and literature.

As Juárez studied more and more, a new plan took shape. Instead of becoming a priest, he decided to serve his people by becoming active in government. With this as his goal, Juárez finished his seminary studies and enrolled in law school at the Institute of Arts and Science in Oaxaca. After three years of intensive schooling, Benito Juárez became an assistant professor at the Institute. The beginning of his political career came when he was also elected to the Oaxaca city council.

The next year, 1832, Juárez was elected to the state legislature, and his fame soon began to spread throughout the area. Juárez was admired for being thoughtful, hard-working, and honest, but most of all, he became known for supporting laws that were fair to every citizen, and for seeing that the laws were carried out.

Mexico was still in distress and confusion. The country had won its independence from Spain in 1821, but it wasn't truly free of Spanish control. There was a national legislature, and many state legislatures as well. Although representatives to the national and state legislatures met, debated, and passed laws, the laws didn't change anything, because they didn't apply to the army, the church, and the ruling upper class. Again and again, local heroes led rebellions against one state government or another, and each time, they were defeated. The Mexican people continued to suffer.

Some of the leaders of these rebellions were just political bosses who put together a ragtag army, while others were fanatics with dreams of glory and power. Still others were corrupt bullies or fast-talking con artists. There were a few leaders who had good intentions, but they had no practical way of making their wonderful promises come true.

Benito Juárez was not like any of these people. He wasn't a brilliant speaker or a glamorous figure, and he always wore simple, dull clothing, not a colorful uniform with shiny buttons, ribbons, and decorations. He led no army and made no grand promises, yet his fine reputation grew. As a lawyer and as a representative, he concentrated on what mattered most.

What, Juárez asked himself, do the people of the villages need?

The answer was the chance to rise from poverty. They needed money to improve their farms, and a way to get their crops to other people. The few roads that linked the villages were no better than muddy tracks filled with stones. Juárez believed that one of the key answers to the problems of Mexico was roads, so the villagers could get to the big cities and sell their crops.

Juárez also believed that Mexico needed a constitution that guaranteed equal rights for everyone under the law, and he favored a bill of rights similar to the one enjoyed by the citizens of the United States. Throughout his life, Juárez fought hard for his ideals. At different times he served Mexico as Deputy to the National Congress, Minister of Justice, Governor of Oaxaca, Chief Justice, and Minister of the Interior. Finally, in 1861, Benito Juárez was elected President of Mexico. Even then, he and his wife, Margarita (one of the daughters of Don Antonio Maza, the man who had taken Benito into his home when he was a 12-year-old runaway), lived simply in the presidential mansion.

Juárez's career wasn't a steady climb to success. There were times when he left government service entirely, his way of showing his disgust at the corrupt, criminal dictators who gained power. Twice, these dictators drove Juárez from Mexico because he refused to join their evil rule. The people loved and honored Juárez because of this, and welcomed him home each time he returned.

Benito Juárez was President of Mexico during the United States' Civil War and a great ally of Abraham Lincoln's government. Juárez hated all slavery, so he refused to trade with the Confederacy, even though it meant refusing money that Mexico badly needed. Doing the right thing was more important to Juárez than making money.

Some Mexican politicians had other ideas. They saw a way to gain great wealth and power by being allies of the Confederacy. They planned to set up an independent empire in northern Mexico and let the Confederate armies use it as a safe zone. Juárez's enemies told the Confederate leaders, "You will be free to attack the Union forces and then escape to this zone. The U.S. government will not be able to follow you over the border into Mexico. Crossing the border means going to war with Mexico and all our European allies, and that is something President Lincoln will not do." Juárez's enemies also hoped this plan would give them enough power to overthrow President Juárez's constitutional government.

Juárez, supported by the Mexican people, defeated the plotters, however, and Mexico remained a strong friend of Lincoln.

Juárez remained President of Mexico until he died, in 1872. He had wanted to retire, but the people saw him as their best hope for honest government, and they re-elected him again and again. Through all the years he spent as president, Juárez never stopped trying to improve the lives of the poor and uneducated. He succeeded in having a railroad system built from the coast to Mexico's capital, Mexico City, and he fought long and hard for a law guaranteeing a free education for every child. His reforms brought the chance for equality to all. Under Juárez, Mexico finally became an independent nation, with the power to decide its own destiny.

"Benito Juárez is Mexico and Mexico is Juárez," said Andres Iduarte, a famous Mexican writer. The poor Zapotec child from the hills grew up to become the living symbol of his country.

Sitting Bull

It was a moonless night, dark enough for the Sioux warriors to surprise their enemies, the Crows.

Slow stood silently as his father rode away without him. They had named him Slow when he was small because he had spoken slowly, eaten slowly, and grown slowly. Now he had seen 14 winters and he was ready to earn a warrior's name. It was time. He would not be slow to show his courage!

Slow painted his body with red war paint, then he mounted his small gray pony and followed the dusty trail of the warriors. The braves in the war party laughed to see a boy dressed for war, but his father did not laugh. Proudly, he gave his brave son his own "coup" stick. The laughter stopped, for every warrior knew that to touch an enemy with this stick took as much courage as to kill!

Silently, they waited as the Crows came closer and closer. Slow could hardly wait, and when the signal finally came, he raced like lightning, ahead of the others. His heart pounded as he leaned forward and struck a retreating Crow warrior. "On-hey!" he shouted. "I, Slow, have conquered him!"

Soon, the battle was done. The Crows had been defeated, and at dawn, the Sioux braves returned to their village. They had horses, weapons, and a new warrior. Slow sat tall and proud on his new bay horse with a gold eagle feather in his hair. The bright feather showed that he had counted his first coup.

That night, the drums beat a song of victory. When his father gave him a warrior's name, the boy danced wildly with happiness. From that night on, he was called Sitting Bull, and in the years to come, he would make that name famous.

Sitting Bull's people, the Sioux, were always on the move, following the great herds of buffalo across the wide plains of the Dakota country. Buffalo meat fed them, buffalo hides covered their tepees, buffalo skins made robes, shields, and drums, and buffalo bones and horns made cups, dishes, tools, and toys. Buffalo ribs made sleds and buffalo chips fueled their fires. No part of the buffalo was wasted. For the Sioux, the buffalo was the "giver of life."

Hunting buffalo was dangerous but exciting, and Sitting Bull was always ready to ride after the shaggy, hump-backed beasts. He was always ready for battle, too! The Sioux did not welcome strangers to their hunting grounds and fought anyone who dared to cross Sioux lands. As Sitting Bull grew to manhood, he counted coup many times and captured many fine horses and guns. It was not long before he wore the feathers and buffalo-horn hat of the warrior society, the Strong Hearts.

Sitting Bull was wounded badly one night in a fierce battle against the Crows, but pain did not stop him. He rushed forward and killed the Crows' chief! From that time on, Sitting Bull walked with a limp, but his bravery was rewarded. At their victory dance, the warriors made him chief of the Strong Hearts!

In time, Sitting Bull became chief of his tribe, the Hunkpapa, one of the many Sioux tribes that lived on the Great Plains. The Hunkpapas held the best hunting grounds, and for a long time, they saw little of the white man's wagons. Other tribes of the great Sioux nation were not so lucky, however. To the east and the south, scattered tribes of Sioux had seen wagons belonging to miners, settlers, and soldiers ruin their hunting grounds. Their arrows could not hold back the endless stream of covered wagons.

Some Indians began to take up the white man's ways, but many decided to leave their lands and head northwest. Sitting Bull could not turn his back on his Indian brothers, and his people shared food, clothing, and tepees with the tribes that came north.

With time came more trouble. Now the wagons began to travel through Hunkpapa territory, and many people came to settle on Sioux land. After them came soldiers with guns that roared like thundering herds of buffalo. The soldiers built forts to protect the new settlers.

Time after time, Sioux war parties attacked the wagon trains, but still, the wagons kept coming. In the summer of 1867, the scattered tribes of the Sioux nation gathered together to save their land. Many chiefs sat together at the council fire. For the first time in their long history, they had to choose one mighty chief to lead them all. Sitting Bull's fame had spread to the tepees of many tribes. He was a fearless fighter; yet he had shown kindness to the poor and homeless. All the chiefs agreed that Sitting Bull was the one to lead them.

Sitting Bull was proud to wear the beautiful chief's headdress of black and white eagle feathers. Each feather stood for a brave deed done by the best warriors of the Sioux nation. Now, the headdress was a sign of their joining together to serve the whole Sioux nation. Sitting Bull knew it would be his duty to see that his people were not hungry. He knew if he spoke for war, they would fight, and if he spoke for peace, they would follow.

He wanted nothing to do with the white men. He did not want war or friendship; he only wanted his people to be left alone. The government in Washington was troubled by the fighting with the Great Plains Indians, so a new treaty was made in 1868 in Laramie. This agreement gave the Sioux a large territory of their own in the Black Hills. Every hill from north of the Platte River and east of the Big Horn Mountains was Indian land.

With the signing of the treaty, Sitting Bull's hopes soared like an eagle! Now, he thought, perhaps the wagons will never again trample the grass of the Sioux hunting grounds. At last the Northern Plains were peaceful. In their sacred Black Hills, the Sioux sang songs of joy to the Great Spirit. Sitting Bull looked out across the plains as the tribes scattered to their old hunting grounds. He knew that peace was the greatest victory a chief could win for his people, and he prayed that the peace would last.

But in less than six winters, the promises made at Laramie had been broken. The cry of "Gold! There's gold in the Black Hills!" went out, and nothing would hold back the miners with their dreams of riches. The treaty meant little to them.

Now, Bluecoats rode into the sacred lands, and word came that the American government wanted to buy the Black Hills. "Never!" said Sitting Bull. "This land belongs to the Sioux. If the outsiders try to take it, we will fight!" Puffs of smoke sent signals across the plains, and soon, every trail led to the camp of Sitting Bull. Never before had so many Indians gathered together. Thousands of Sioux, Cheyenne, Arapaho, and Blackfoot warriors sang songs of war.

For many days, the warriors danced the sacred Sun Dance. As the tom-toms beat, Sitting Bull danced and prayed until finally, he could dance no more. His men carried him to his tepee where he had a strange dream. In it he saw Bluecoats falling from the sky into the Indians' camp, a sign of a great victory for his people.

Soon afterward, when General George Crook led more than a thousand men into the Rosebud Valley, Indian scouts saw the dust rise from the long line of soldiers. The signals for war came to Sitting Bull's camp. The warriors were ready and they rode out to battle.

General Crook never reached Sitting Bull's camp. By

sundown, many Bluecoats had fallen, and General Crook rode away in defeat.

Sitting Bull warned his men that more Bluecoats would come. "This was not the battle in my dream," he said. "The Bluecoats will come into our camp. We must stay together. We must be ready."

Seven days passed and Sitting Bull moved his camp to the valley of the Little Big Horn River. A city of tepees stood side by side in wide circles. At noon on the eighth day, the peace was broken with a cry of alarm. Warriors on the hillside shouted, "Bluecoats! Many Bluecoats!"

Colonel George A. Custer led the fateful charge. He had been warned that his men were badly outnumbered, but Custer had dreams of great glory. He wanted this battle to make him famous, and he was determined to defeat the mighty Chief Sitting Bull.

Bullets and arrows flew and war cries filled the air. The battle was fierce and terrible, but it did not last long. In a very short time, Colonel Custer and all his men were dead. By late summer, the Indians had killed more than a thousand soldiers. Sitting Bull knew that these were great victories, but he also knew that more Bluecoats would come. Bluecoats on ponies, Bluecoats on foot, Bluecoats with cannons would come endlessly onto Indian lands.

With each moon, the buffalo were harder to find, yet Sitting Bull's people had to be fed. Though it made his heart heavy to think of leaving his land, Sitting Bull knew that he and his people must go. At the council fire, the chiefs could not agree. Some wanted to stay and fight, while others said they would go south. Before long, the tribes had scattered in many directions.

Sitting Bull decided to lead the Hunkpapas north to Canada. With the winter coming upon them, they sadly left their sacred Black Hills.

In Canada, where the English ruled, Sitting Bull found peace for his people, but planting crops and living in one place was not the way of the Sioux. Now they had no hunting ground of their own, but they could not become farmers. To the south, the Bluecoats had burned the grass the buffalo ate, and they killed the great animals by the thousands. Sitting Bull's people were hungry and poor. As food became more scarce, they longed for their old life on the plains. Sitting Bull feared his people would die of hunger.

In 1878, messengers came to Canada from the government in Washington with new promises of peace, food, and a reservation. Sitting Bull did not believe them—he was sure that if he crossed the line, they would kill him—but as the seasons passed, he faced the sad truth. His people were starving, and as chief, he had to lead them back into the land of their birth.

On a hot July day in 1881, Sitting Bull rode into Fort Buford in North Dakota to surrender. He was no longer young and strong, and his tired face showed the hardships of the long, difficult years. Sitting Bull felt a great sadness as he stood on Dakota ground. His young men would not live as hunters and do brave deeds. The government would close them up in a reservation, and his people would have to travel the white man's path.

"Let it be known," he sadly said, "that I, Sitting Bull, was the last man of my people to lay down my gun."

For two years, the great leader of the Sioux nation was kept a prisoner of the government while what remained of the Hunkpapa tribe was sent to the Standing Rock Reservation. Finally, Sitting Bull was allowed to return to his people. He found them hungry and cold. Long seasons without rain had turned the soil to dust, and there were no buffalos for meat. There was nowhere to go.

The government had promised the Indians cattle, tools, and wagons. Again, Sitting Bull reminded the government agent, James McLaughlin, of these promises, but McLaughlin would do little to help. To McLaughlin and the Bluecoats, Sitting Bull was nothing but a troublemaker, so in 1885, McLaughlin sent Sitting Bull to travel with Buffalo Bill's Wild West Show. The name of Sitting Bull was known throughout the land, and many people were curious to see what he looked like. "Now," McLaughlin thought, "the Indians won't have their leader around to stir them up!"

In city after city, people packed the halls to see the old chief. Buffalo Bill wanted to take Sitting Bull to England, but the chief had had enough of shows. He was not happy on the reservation, but he was not happy in the white man's world, either, so he returned to his people.

At Standing Rock, Sitting Bull found new trouble. Conditions had grown worse, and hunger and sickness were sweeping through Indian reservations all over the West. Far away, in Nevada, a Paiute Indian called Wovoca dreamed of new hope for all Indians. He said that soon all the dead warriors would rise up, the buffalo would return, and the white men would leave the Indians' land forever.

The desperate people needed such a hope. Wovoca's word spread from one reservation to the next, and day after day, Indians danced and sang the sacred songs of the Ghost Dance. They thought it would bring back the old times of happiness and plenty. Sitting Bull did not really believe such a dream, but many of his people did, so he did not stop them from dancing.

Week after week, the loud drums and sad songs of the Ghost Dance echoed, like war songs, across the plains. The settlers were frightened, and the Bluecoats were worried, too.

By now, in Standing Rock, Indian had turned against Indian, with some Indians working as soldiers to keep order among their own people. The Bluecoats believed Sitting Bull would lead the Indians to war again, and they were ready for an uprising. On a cold winter night in December of 1890, McLaughlin sent a large party of Indian soldiers to bring Sitting Bull back, dead or alive! Sitting Bull was pulled from his bed and out of his cabin.

Shouting in anger, his warriors rushed to save their chief while the Indian soldiers pushed Sitting Bull toward his horse. Suddenly, there was a single gunshot . . . then another, and another!

When it was all over, 14 men were dead. One of them was Sitting Bull.

With Sitting Bull's death, the Ghost Dances ended, and not long afterward, the Indian war drums were silenced at the Battle of Wounded Knee. Towns and cities grew where tepees had stood, and trains rumbled across the trails where buffalo had grazed. The old ways were gone, but the name of Sitting Bull was not forgotten.

Theodore Roosevelt

The first Roosevelt came to America in 1649 and settled on Manhattan Island. A farmer with little money, he had a reputation as an honest, hard-working man. With each new generation of Roosevelts, the family fortunes grew, but the sense of honor and responsibility to others never changed. It was into this long tradition that Theodore Roosevelt was born, on October 27, 1858, a member of the seventh generation of Roosevelts born in Manhattan.

Teddy was the second child of Theodore, Sr., and Martha Bulloch Roosevelt. Mr. Roosevelt and his four brothers were successful in banking, real estate, and business, and the family, which also included three-year-old Anna, lived in a comfortable house with many servants. All the Roosevelts lived within a few blocks of one another, and their families were very close. For the Roosevelt children there were always cousins to play with, and aunts and uncles visiting back and forth.

Almost from the day they were born, Anna, Teddy, then Elliott and Corinne, learned Roosevelt traditions. Those included prayers with Papa in the sitting room every morning, and days filled with lessons, physical exercise, visits, and play. In the evening, the children waited in the library until Papa came home, then they rushed to greet him and follow him upstairs to his dressing room. There, they were allowed to watch him shave and change into evening clothes. Even when Mr. and Mrs. Roosevelt dined at home, they always dressed formally for dinner.

Teddy's mother had lived on a vast plantation in Georgia when she was a girl. Her family was as important in the South as the Roosevelts were in the North. Martha Roosevelt was an extraordinary person, and Theodore Roosevelt's character was shaped equally by both parents. From his father, he acquired a sense of civic duty and a strict code of honor. Mr. Roosevelt was one of the organizers of The Children's Aid Society, as well as the Newsboy's Lodging House, which provided beds and meals to stray children. He also was a founder of the New York Orthopedic Hospital, the Metropolitan Museum of Art, and the American Museum of Natural History. In addition, he spent a good deal of time collecting money from friends and associates for other worthwhile charities.

Mrs. Roosevelt was a warm and outgoing woman, who enjoyed telling stories, especially about her heroic ancestors and relations. Teddy loved to hear Mama talk about Grandpa hunting foxes and wildcats; of duels and bear-chases; of brave sailors and daring explorers. The boy dreamed of one day doing brave things himself, but Teddy's dreams seemed to have little chance of coming true. Young Theodore Roosevelt suffered serious attacks of asthma, and each frightening attack made him wheeze and gasp for air. Teddy felt as if he were choking, and his parents often worried that their small, frail boy would not live to manhood. The attacks came every week or two, without warning, and Teddy was constantly terrified that one might start at any time.

The asthma began in 1862, when Teddy was four years old. The Civil War had erupted the year before, and the whole family was deeply affected by it. The war kept Mr. Roosevelt away for many months at a time. He had worked out a plan for Union soldiers to send some of their pay home each month so that their families would have a small, steady income. This plan to send home, or allot, part of a soldier's pay had never been done before, and President Lincoln thought it was an excellent idea. He asked Mr. Roosevelt to organize the project, visit Army camps, and sign up the troops. Mr. Roosevelt spent the rest of the war years at this work, and it was a great success. In fact, the allotment plan became a permanent part of the United States military payroll system.

The Roosevelts were strongly pro-Union, with one exception—Teddy's mother, whose brothers were in the Confederate Navy. In addition, Martha's mother and sister lived with her, and they were also pro-Confederacy. They didn't talk about it in front of the Roosevelt clan, but they acted on it in secret. Whenever Mr. Roosevelt was away, the three women packaged clothing to be sent to friends in the South. Teddy, his brother, and his sisters didn't really understand what was going on. All they knew was that it was a secret from the other Roosevelts and everyone outside the family. The children liked the idea of a mystery, yet they were confused by the divided loyalties in their own home.

Though the war made an impression on the children, it did not change their lives very much. Part of every day was spent with Aunt Anna Bulloch, who tutored all the Roosevelt children. This was another family tradition, and none of them ever attended public schools. Aunt Anna taught them reading, writing, and arithmetic. Teddy was terrible at arithmetic, and he continued to dislike it all his life, but reading and writing were always a pleasure for him.

The sickly little boy couldn't do many of the physical things other children did as he was often confined to the house, but he found a way to escape his closed world through reading. One day he wandered into the family library and opened a large book. The book's title was *Missionary Travels and Researches in South Africa,* by David Livingstone. Most of the words in the book were too hard for the boy to read, but he found the pictures fascinating. There were zebras, hippopotamuses, elephants, and insects. The beginning of a lifelong interest in wildlife, Teddy was fascinated and carried the book around for weeks. Right away, he decided he would be a naturalist when he grew up, and he would contribute to Papa's American Museum of Natural History.

Young Theodore Roosevelt planned to learn everything there was to know about nature. Nothing seemed more romantic or exciting than to travel to far-off places, meet all kinds of people, and collect specimens of rare and beautiful plants and animals. Until he could do that, however, he would find adventure in books. He read natural histories, exciting stories, tales of the American frontier, myths and legends.

Of course, Teddy did not have to spend all of his time indoors, reading. When he was well enough, he played with the other Roosevelt children on the family's back porch, and he was encouraged to run errands around the neighborhood. It was on one of those errands that seven-year-old Teddy saw something that made a deep impression on him. As he later wrote, "I was walking up Broadway, and as I passed the market to which I used sometimes to be sent before breakfast to get strawberries, I suddenly saw a dead seal laid out on a slab of wood. That seal filled me with every possible feeling of romance and adventure."

Teddy came back to see the seal day after day. He looked at it, asked questions about it, measured it up, down, and around, then he began to write a natural history based on his observations. He wanted to own the animal and display it as a prize specimen. Although Teddy didn't get the whole seal, he was given the skull. With two of his cousins, he promptly started "The Roosevelt Museum of Natural History." The collection's main attraction was the seal skull, but their museum also had field mice, snapping turtles, snakes, and a variety of insects.

Most of Teddy's collecting was done during summer vacations. Every year, the Roosevelt family rented a house in the country, and these vacations were special for the Roosevelt children. They were free to run and play outdoors, fish, hike, pick berries, and ride horses. Mr. Roosevelt was a fine horseman, and he made sure the children also had ponies to ride.

Horseback-riding was an activity that Teddy enjoyed all of his life. Many years later, he organized the First United States Volunteer Cavalry Regiment, which was called the Rough Riders. He also bought and worked on two cattle ranches in the Dakota Territory.

In the summer of 1868, when Teddy was nine-and-a-half years old, he began to keep a diary. This was another habit that stayed with him for the rest of his life. In addition, Theodore Roosevelt wrote many books of history, journals about his hunting trips and ranch life, thousands of letters, and a long autobiography.

In the spring of 1869, Teddy, Anna, Corinne, Elliott, and their parents traveled to Europe. There were a number of reasons for the trip. Mr. and Mrs. Roosevelt felt it would be educational for the children to visit museums, castles, and other historical places, and it would be an opportunity to meet important people and to learn some French, German, and Italian language skills. Another reason for the trip was that Mrs. Roosevelt's brothers, who she had not seen since the beginning of the Civil War, were living in England. Martha's brothers, Irvine and James Bulloch, had fought for the South. At the end of the war, they refused to give up their loyalty to the defeated Confederacy, nor would they swear allegiance to the United States. As a result, they were not allowed to return to America.

For Mrs. Roosevelt, the reunion was joyful, but for Teddy, it was unbelievably exciting. To him, the Bulloch brothers were dashing military heroes. In later years, the grown-up Teddy encouraged James Bulloch to write a book titled *The Secret Service of the Confederate States in Europe*. In turn, Uncle James supplied valuable information for young Roosevelt's own first book, a naval history of the War of 1812. This book was begun when Teddy was a student at Harvard University.

The Roosevelts' trip to Europe lasted a little more than a year, and during that time, the family visited England, Scotland, France, Germany, Italy, Austria, and Switzerland. Into Teddy's journal went all kinds of information, especially about nature. One entry, made in France, read: "We saw a tree 1,400 years old. We saw a stream of pure and cold water. We had such a happy time."

Another entry, from France, said: "We went in the park where on a sand bank we made tunnels 10 paces long. After dinner we went to the rocks where we jumped over crevasses and ran in them and had such fun. In one of our rambles we saw very fresh traces of a deer."

It was clear from his writings that 11-year-old Teddy enjoyed those parts of the trip that were spent outdoors, exploring and playing. The rest of the trip—visiting museums, art galleries, and churches—was less of a pleasure for all of the Roosevelt children.

Mr. and Mrs. Roosevelt had hoped the European tour would be more than educational. They thought it might cure Teddy's asthma, but he still had frequent attacks, which continued when the family was back home. Even a summer at Oyster Bay, on New York's Long Island shore and one of the boy's favorite places, made no difference in his health.

Desperate to help the youngster, Mr. and Mrs. Roosevelt considered sending Teddy to the Rocky Mountains, where he might breathe easier. People believed that the thin, dry air in the Rockies was good for asthma sufferers. The Roosevelts really did not want to send their young boy so far from home, and Teddy did not want to leave his parents and friends, so Mr. and Mrs.

Roosevelt decided to try one last remedy—physical activity. Teddy's older sister, Anna, had been born with a back problem, and to help her, a doctor recommended body-strengthening exercises. The plan worked.

Because Anna's back had been helped by regular therapy, Mr. and Mrs. Roosevelt hoped the same kind of constant, hard physical exercise might benefit Teddy. One day, Mr. Roosevelt sat down with his son and said, "Theodore, you have the mind, but you have not the body, and without the help of the body the mind cannot go as far as it should. You must *make* your body. It is hard drudgery . . . but I know you will do it." The boy agreed.

Teddy and his mother began going to Mr. John Wood's Gymnasium every day. Mrs. Roosevelt sat, watched, and encouraged the 12-year-old boy. He worked with weights—pushing, pulling, and lifting them until he could do no more. He pounded a punching bag, swung dumbbells, and spent hours practicing on horizontal bars. It was drudgery, as his father said it would be, but the boy never complained or allowed himself to stop. Within a short time, it was clear that the effort was paying off. Week after week passed without an asthma attack. Teddy stayed thin, but his strength grew every day. His arms and legs had a wiry power, even though there were no bulging muscles on them, but his chest expanded greatly. This was proof to his parents, and to him, that his breathing would continue to get easier.

After three months at Wood's Gymnasium, the Roosevelts set up their own gymnasium and weight equipment on the back porch. Teddy could work out there as often and as much as he liked, and the other Roosevelt children could join him any time they wanted to. Plus, Mrs. Roosevelt didn't have to spend her whole day sitting in the gymnasium.

As Teddy's health improved, he was able to do many more things. During the summer of 1871, he spent an energetic vacation in the Adirondack Mountains of New York State, where he swam in the icy streams and rivers, climbed mountains, went hiking for days, and canoed over swift waters. The boy delighted in a feeling of well-being.

Until now, Teddy had felt that a life of active adventure was out of his reach. Suddenly, such a life *was* possible. Realizing this, the youngster plunged into every activity with great energy and interest. He was enthusiastic about learning everything, and doing everything. It was an enthusiasm that would never leave him. When Theodore Roosevelt was President and living in the White House, his zest for life often startled people. On winter evenings, he sometimes went swimming in the freezing Potomac River. He built a gymnasium for his children, and used it as much as they did. He climbed trees, boxed and wrestled with professionals, rode, hunted, and always had a good time. It was as if he was making up for those early years of physical inactivity.

When Teddy was 13, he began to look forward to higher education. He wanted to go to Harvard College, and to prepare himself, he studied long and hard with tutors in English, German, French, and Latin. Teddy also took lessons in taxidermy from John Bell, the man who had stuffed animals for James Audubon, the famed naturalist.

The boy stuffed every specimen he could acquire, but he soon ran out of animals on which to work. To solve the problem, Mr. Roosevelt gave Teddy a double-barreled shotgun and told him to shoot his own specimens in the woods. To his dismay, Teddy couldn't hit anything, while his brother and cousins were successful hunters. In fact, Teddy couldn't even see what they were shooting. He told his father, and Mr. Roosevelt took Teddy for an eye examination.

In his autobiography, President Roosevelt wrote, "Soon afterwards I got my first pair of spectacles, which literally opened an entirely new world to me. I had no idea how beautiful the world was until I got those spectacles. . . . I could not see, and yet was wholly ignorant that I was not seeing."

Once he had glasses, young Roosevelt's interests as a naturalist changed. In the past, he had studied mammals—the larger they were, the better. Now he became a bird-watcher, and this interest never left him. As President of the United States, Roosevelt kept a complete list of the birds he saw on the White House grounds, 56 species in all.

Theodore Roosevelt's teen years were busy, happy, and educational. He and his family spent a year traveling in Europe and North Africa, and Teddy brought back a fine collection of stuffed birds. Then, in September 1876, when Teddy was almost 18, he entered Harvard.

The young Roosevelt stood five feet eight inches, and he was still thin, although the barrel chest of his later years was starting to develop. As a college student, Theodore got excellent marks and was on the boxing and wrestling teams. He also ran track, rowed, and taught Sunday school. He even found time and energy to join several college clubs, to attend concerts, parties and lectures, and to begin work on his first history book.

The pleasure of those years was diminished when Mr. Roosevelt died, in February 1878. For the rest of his life, Theodore tried to be the fine man his father hoped he would be. When he was graduated from Harvard with honors, Theodore enrolled at Columbia University Law School, in New York City. After a year, however, a growing interest in politics led the young man to run for the New York State Assembly, an election he won. It was during his third term as assemblyman that Roosevelt suffered a double tragedy. His mother and wife died on the same day. Filled with grief, the young man left politics and went out West.

After two years as a cattleman in the Dakota Territory, Roosevelt came back to New York and resumed his political career.

He served on the City Service Commission, as New York City's police commissioner, and as Assistant Secretary of the Navy under President William McKinley. Roosevelt gained national fame in 1898, during the Spanish-American War, when as commander of the Rough Riders, he fought bravely and led his troops well. On his return, he was greeted as a hero, and easily won the election for Governor of New York State.

A year later, Roosevelt ran for Vice President with President McKinley. The McKinley-Roosevelt ticket won, and in March 1901, Theodore became Vice President of the United States. Six months later, he became President when McKinley was assassinated. Theodore Roosevelt was 42 years old, the youngest man to become President of the United States.

During his eight years in office, Roosevelt was an active, vigorous President, and under his leadership, the United States government began to conserve the nation's huge natural resources. The number of national parks doubled, and Roosevelt's administration also established 16 national monument areas, 51 wildlife refuges, and added 125 million acres to the national forests.

His involvement in foreign policy was equally vigorous. Roosevelt believed that the United States, as a strong, young country, should be an important world power. For example, President Roosevelt declared that the United States would actively protect Latin America against any interference from Europe. President Roosevelt believed that the United States should use its prestige and power to help maintain world peace, and during the war between Russia and Japan in 1905, Roosevelt offered his services as mediator, a person who tries to settle the differences between two conflicting parties. He succeeded in bringing about the war's end, and for this, he was awarded the Nobel Peace Prize.

When Roosevelt left the Presidency, in 1909, he intended to enjoy the rest of his life hunting, collecting specimens for museums, and maintaining an active, productive life. He traveled to

Africa and South America, wrote a number of books, and led the American Historical Society. He could not resist a return to politics, though, and in 1912, he ran for President as an independent candidate, but was defeated.

Until his death, on January 6, 1919, Theodore Roosevelt continued to give freely of his time and talents to the America he loved. He left behind a treasury of writings, political accomplishments, a widespread system of parks and forests, and a reputation as a man of honor, courage, and vision.

INDEX

Boleyn, Queen Anne, 9, 10, 12, 13
Buffalo, 44, 45, 47, 48, 49

Custer, Colonel George A., 47

Edward, King, 13, 15, 16
Elizabeth I, 9–18
  adolescence, 15–16
  childhood, 9–15
  education, 14–16
  Elizabethan Age, 17–18
  imprisoned, 16–17
  life in the castle, 11, 12
  loses mother, 13
  parents, 9, 10, 12, 13
  Queen of England, 17–18
  siblings, 9, 13, 15, 16–17
  stepmothers, 13, 14
  unwilling to marry, 15
England, 9, 17, 18
  rivalry with Spain, 9, 17

Grey, Lady Jane, 16

Henry VIII, 9, 10, 12, 13
  mood swings, 10
  violence, 13, 14
  wish for a son, 10, 12, 13
Henry, Patrick, 19–29
  American Revolution, 28, 29
  childhood, 19–25
  education, 22, 24
  general store, 25, 26
  gift for talking, 22, 23, 26–27, 28
  governor of Virginia, 28
  House of Burgesses, 27, 28
  parents, 19, 20, 21, 22, 25, 26
  political interests, 26, 27, 28
  Saint Andrew's Day, 20, 21
  Scottish background, 20–21
  siblings, 21, 25

Uncle Billy, 23, 24
Virginia Convention, 28

Juárez, Benito, 31–41
   adolescence, 37–38
   childhood, 31–37
   education, 33, 37–39
   orphaned, 32
   Oaxaca, 32, 34, 35–40
   parents, 31, 32
   political career, 39–41
   poverty, 31–34
   presidency, 40, 41
   reforms, 40–41
   siblings 31, 32, 35
   Uncle Bernardino, 32–35
   Zapotec Indians, 32, 33, 36

London, England, 9, 15

Mexico, 31–41
   class system, 36
   Creoles, 36
   independence, 39
   mestizos, 36
   politics, 39
   poverty, 37, 40
   relations with U.S., 40–41
   Spanish rule, 36–37
   Zapotec Indians, 32, 33, 36

Plague, 11

Roosevelt, Theodore, 51–61
   adolescence, 57–59
   ancestors, 51
   asthma, 52, 56–57
   childhood, 51–57
   Civil War, 52–53
   education 53, 58, 59
   family traditions, 51–52, 53
   horseback riding, 55
   Lincoln, President Abraham, 53
   loses father, mother, wife, 59

natural history, love of, 54, 55, 58, 59, 60, 61
  Nobel Prize, 60
  parents, 51, 52, 53, 55, 56, 57
  physical therapy, 57, 58
  political career, 59, 60, 61
  presidency, 58, 59, 60
  Rough Riders, 55, 60
  siblings, 51, 53, 55, 57
  Spanish-American War, 60
  travel, 54–56, 57–58, 60, 61
  writings, 55, 56, 61

Seymour, Queen Jane, 13
Sioux Indians, 43–50
  Battle of Wounded Knee, 50
  battles with Crow Indians, 43
  Ghost Dance, 50
  Hunkpapas, 44, 45, 47–48
  Laramie Treaty, 45–46
  relations with whites, 45–50
  Rosebud Valley, 46
Sitting Bull, 43–50
  adolescence, 43–44
  Battle of Little Big Horn, 47
  Buffalo Bill's Wild West Show, 49
  chief of Hunkpapas, 44
  chief of Sioux, 45
  defends Black Hills, 46
  hunter, 44
  leads tribes to Canada, 47–48
  parents, 43, 44
  "Slow," 43
  Standing Rock Reservation, 48, 49
  surrenders, 48
  warrior, 43, 44, 45–47
  warrior name, 44

Tower of London, 13, 16, 17
Tudor, Queen Mary, 9, 16–17

Windsor Castle, 10